Chopin
FOR EASY PIANO

CONTENTS

Arranged by David Pearl

Cherry Lane Music Company
Director of Publications/Project Editor: Mark Phillips
Project Coordinator: Rebecca Skidmore

ISBN 978-1-60378-212-8

Visit our website at www.cherrylaneprint.com

Etude

Opus 10, No. 3

By Frédéric Chopin

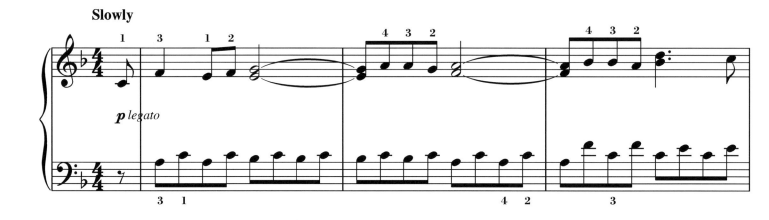

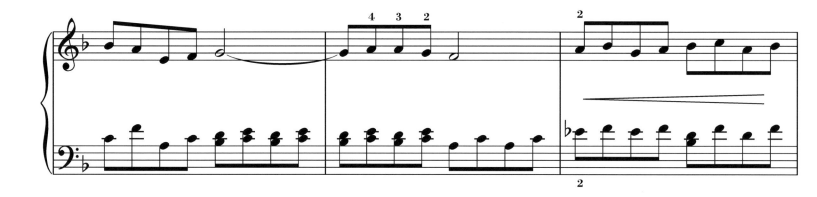

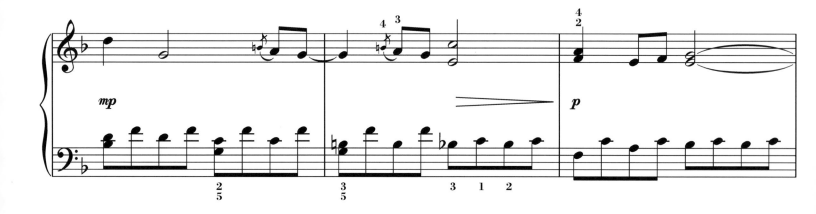

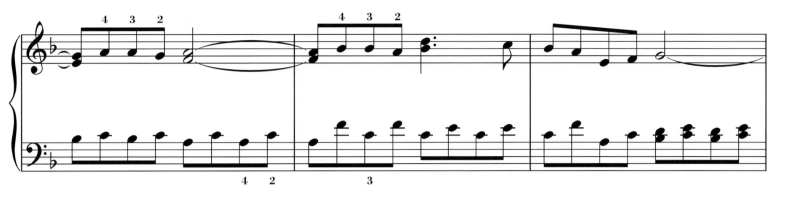

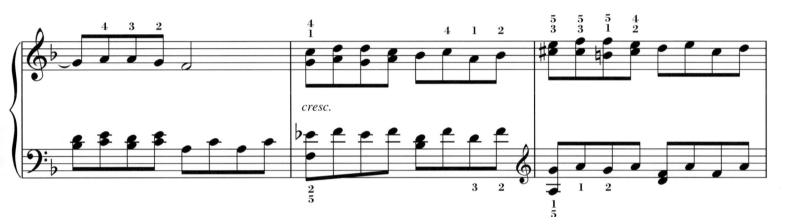

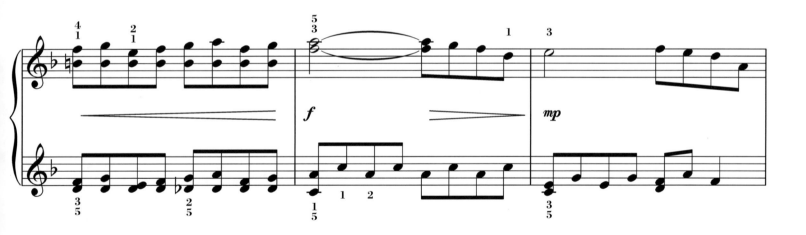

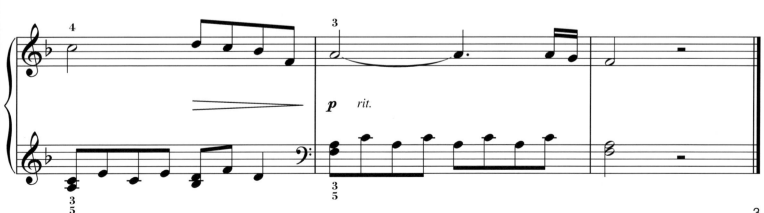

Grande Valse Brillante

Opus 34, No. 1

By Frédéric Chopin

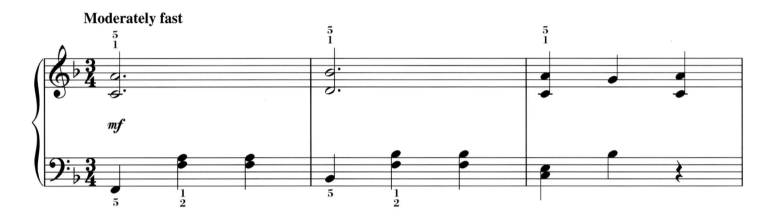

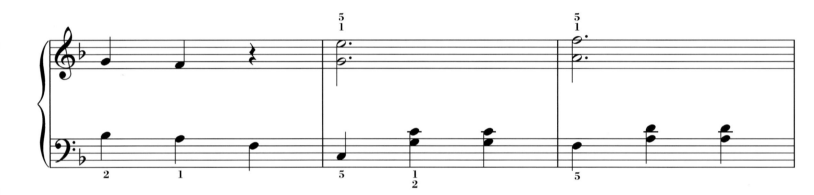

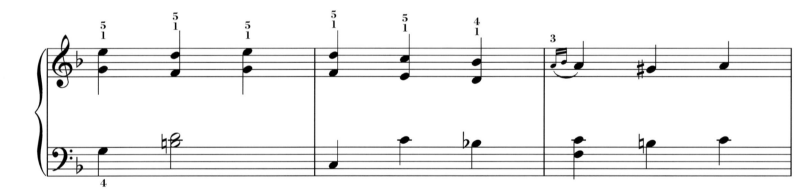

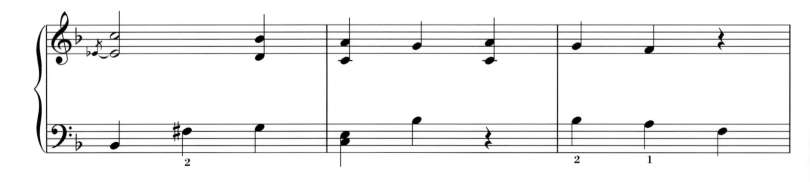

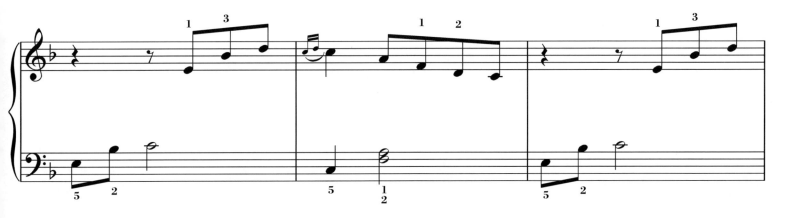

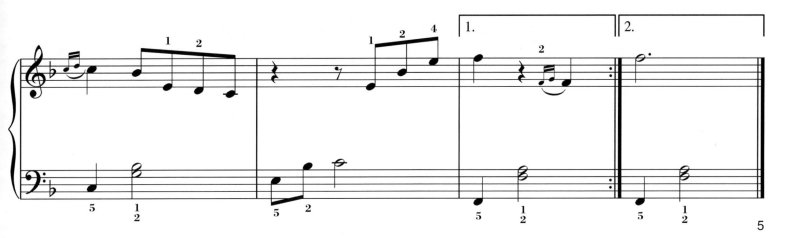

Mazurka No. 25

Opus 33, No. 4

By Frédéric Chopin

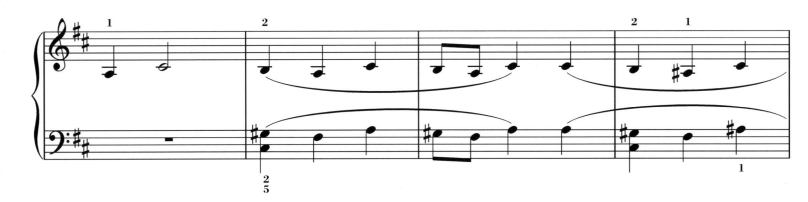

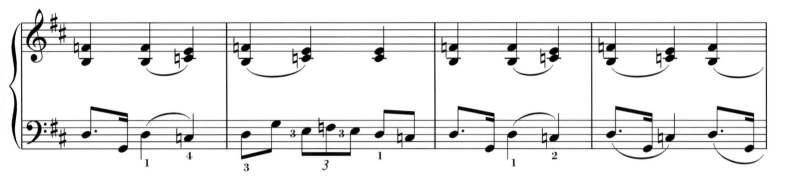

To Coda ⊕

D.S. al Coda

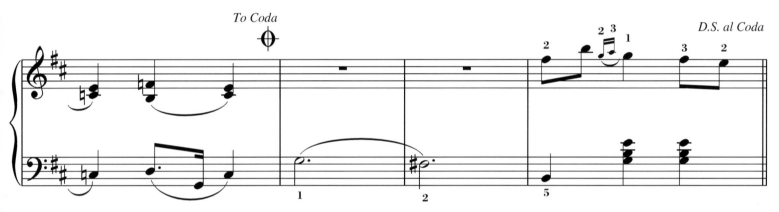

Coda ⊕

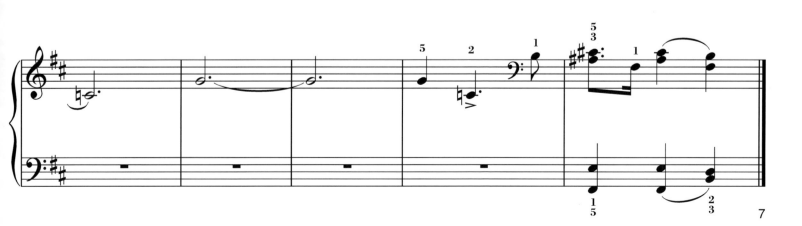

7

Mazurka No. 43

Opus 67, No. 2

By Frédéric Chopin

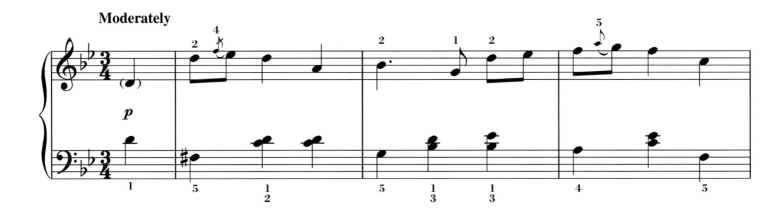

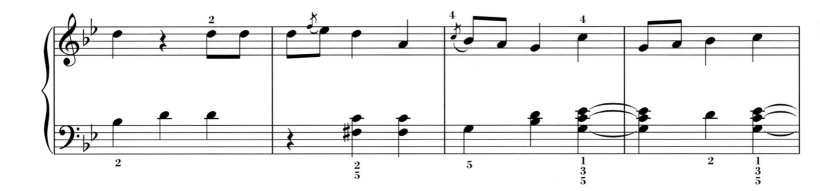

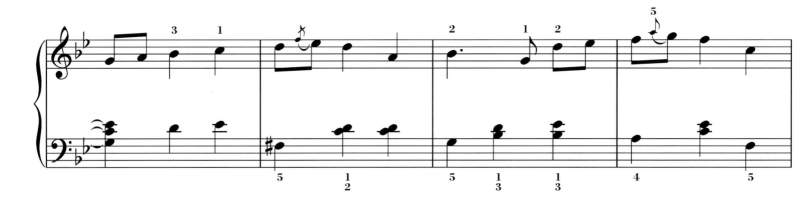

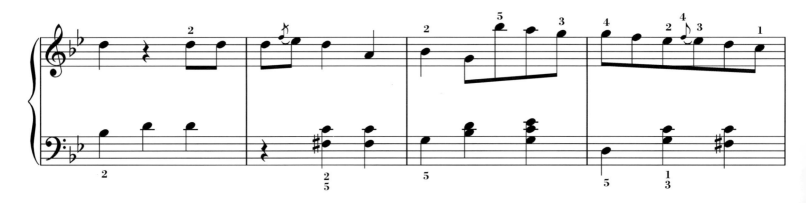

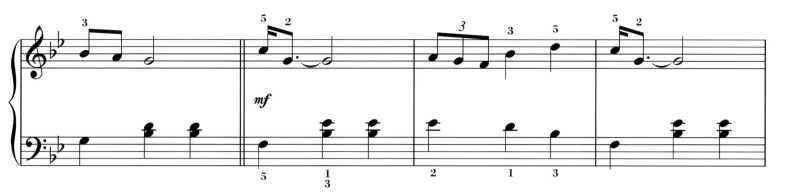

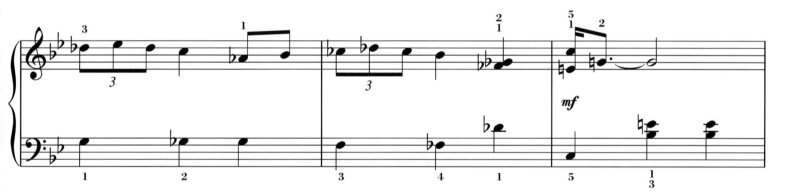

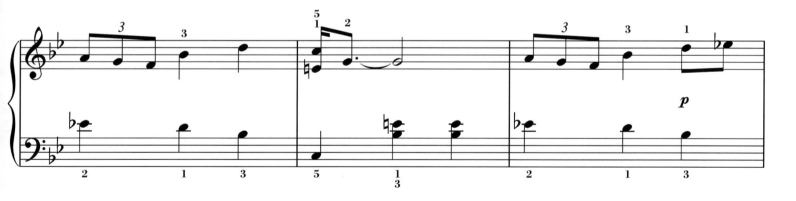

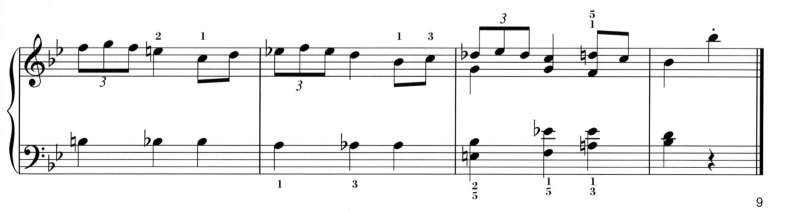

Mazurka No. 47

Opus 68, No. 2

By Frédéric Chopin

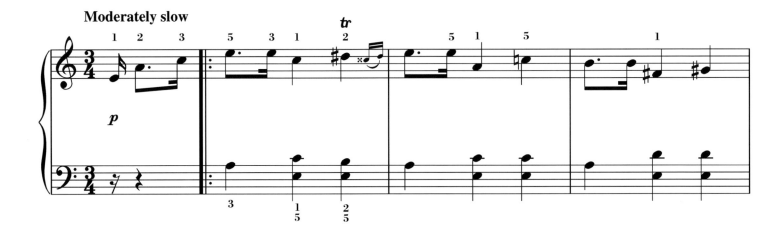

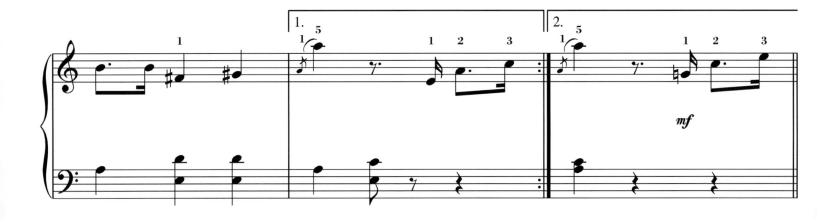

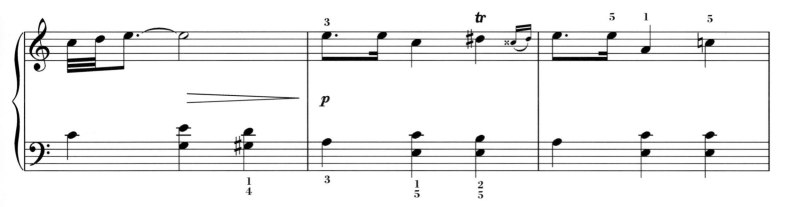

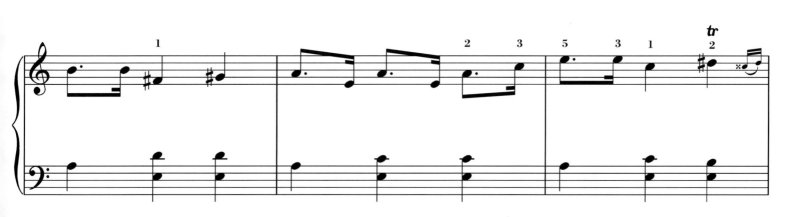

Fantaisie-Impromptu

Moderato Cantabile
Opus 66

By Frédéric Chopin

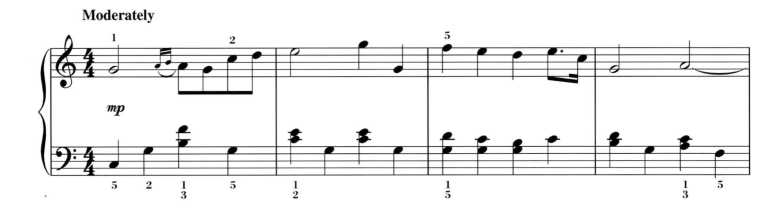

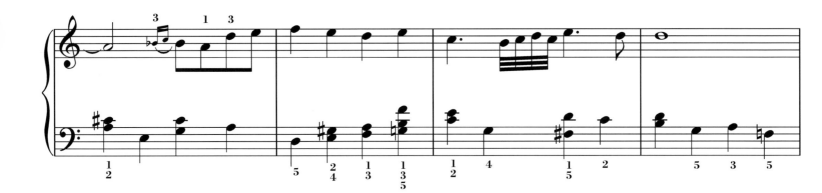

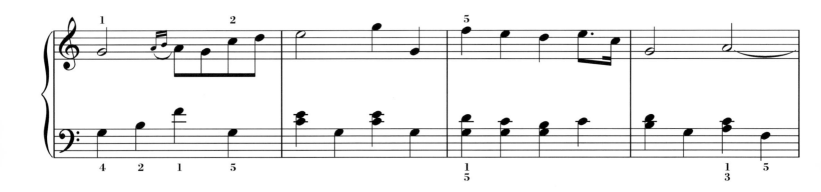

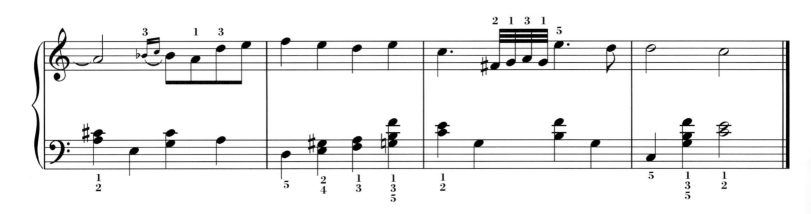

Nocturne No. 2

Opus 9, No. 2

By Frédéric Chopin

Slowly, in 1

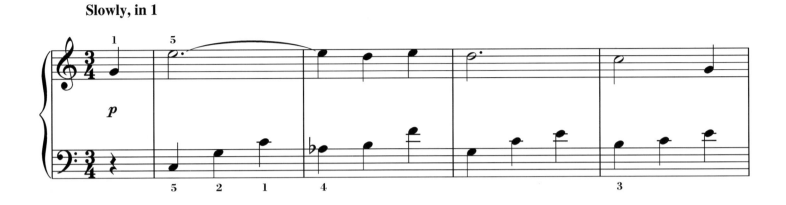

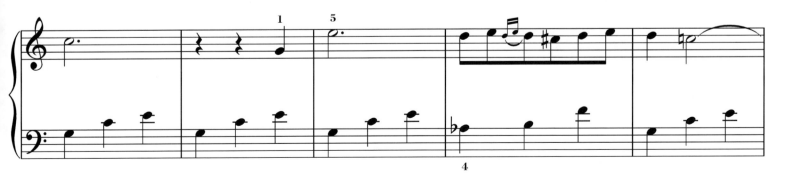

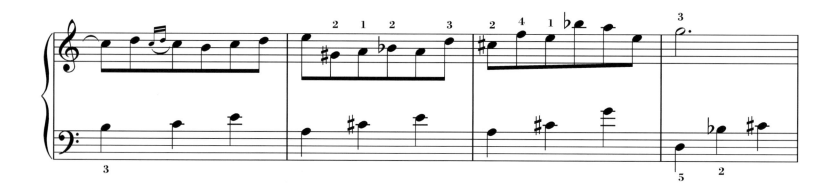

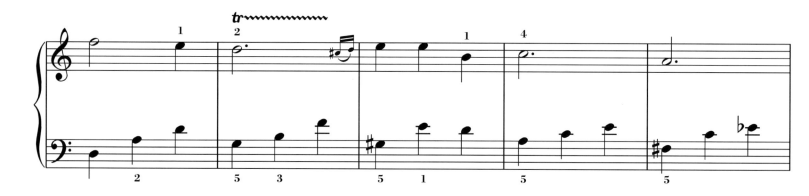

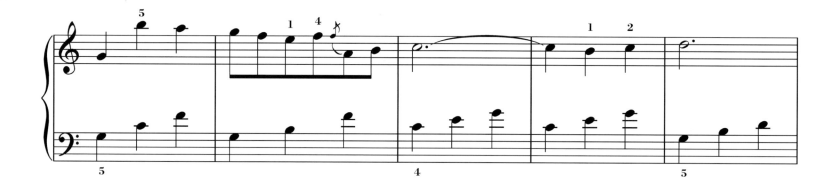

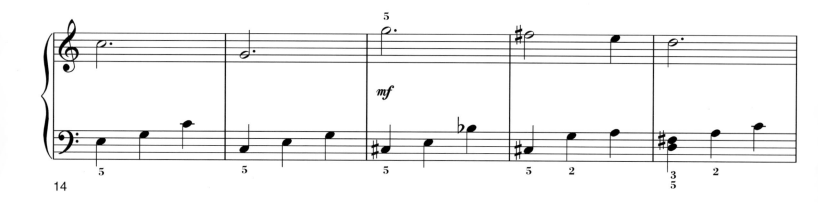

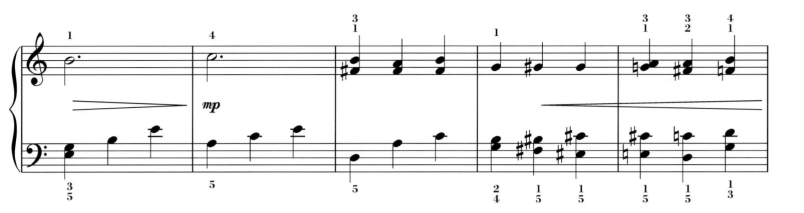

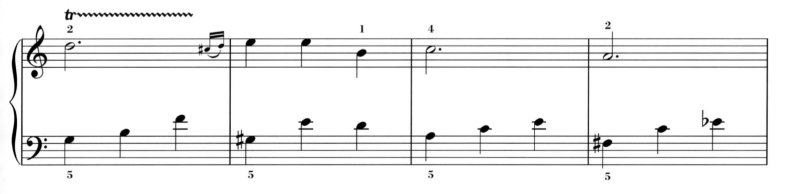

Nocturne No. 11

Opus 37, No. 1

By Frédéric Chopin

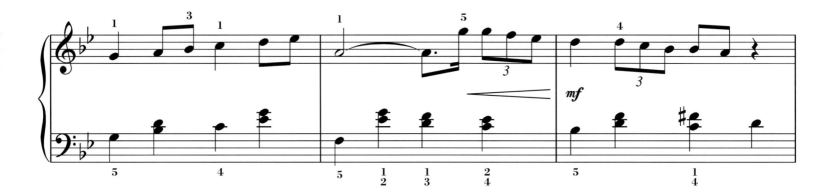

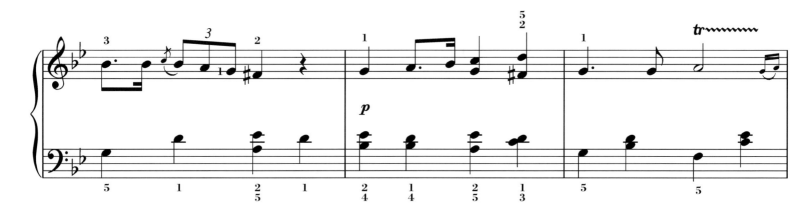

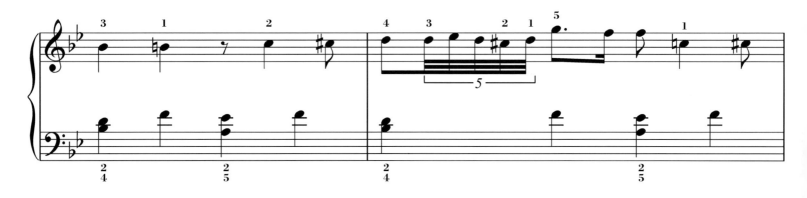

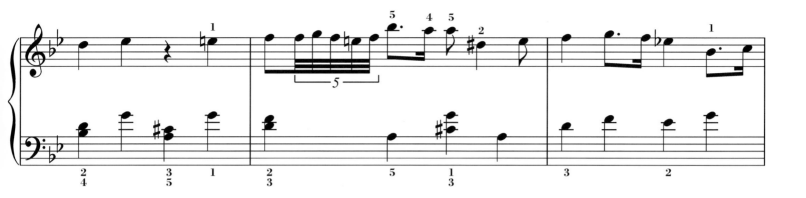

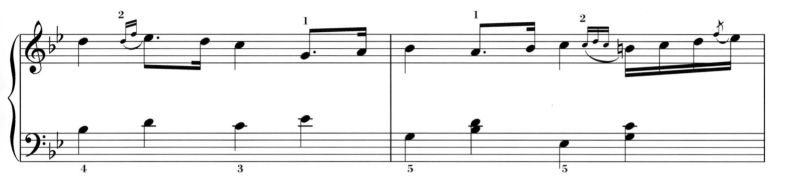

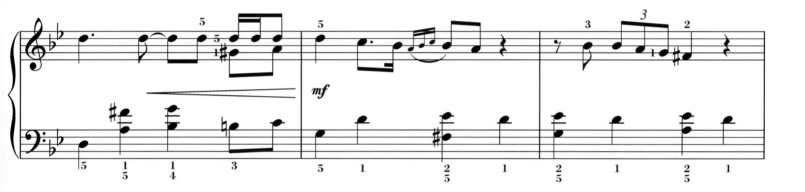

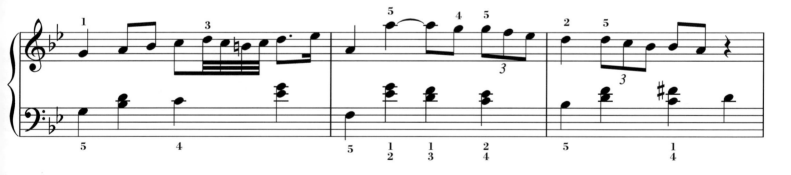

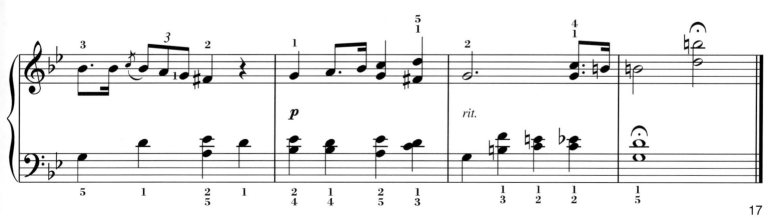

Nocturne No. 15

Opus 55, No. 1

By Frédéric Chopin

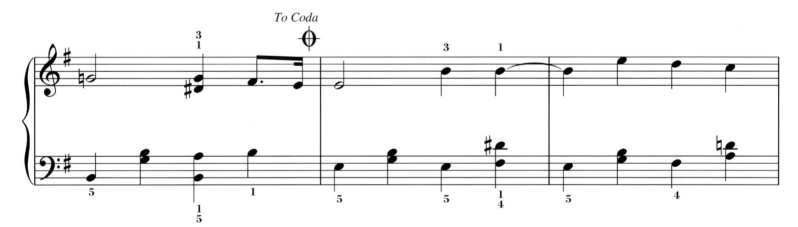

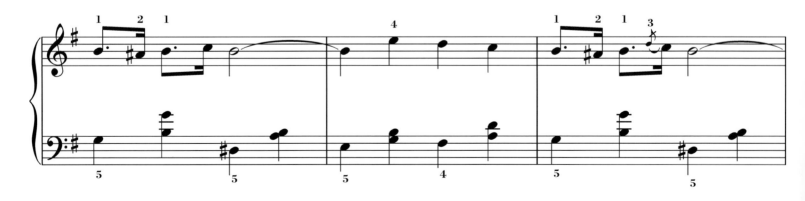

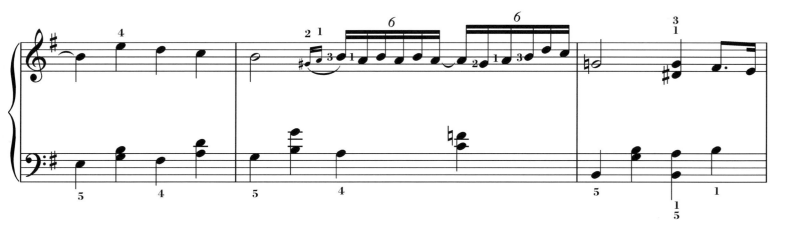

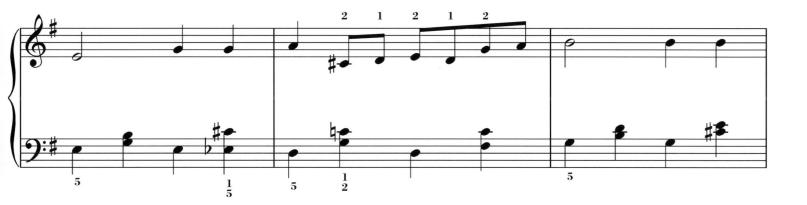

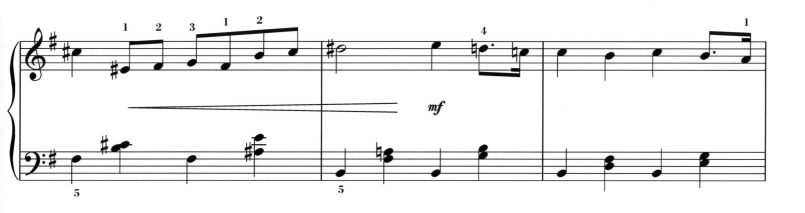

D.S. al Coda

Piano Concerto No. 1

First Movement Theme
Opus 11

By Frédéric Chopin

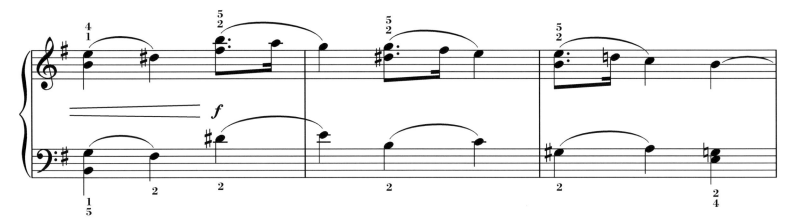

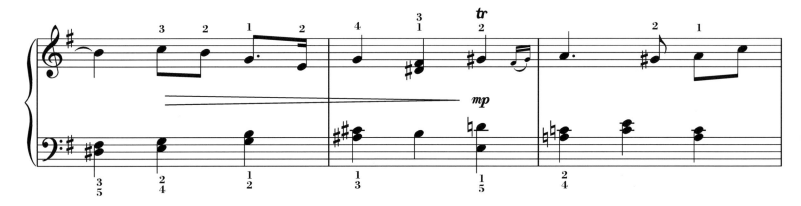

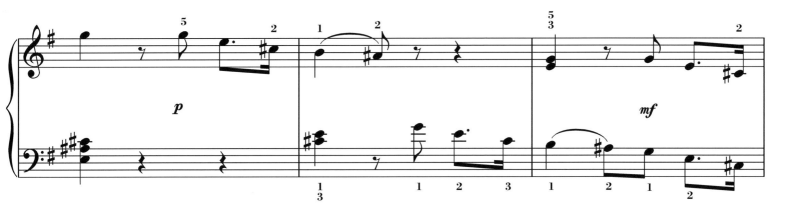

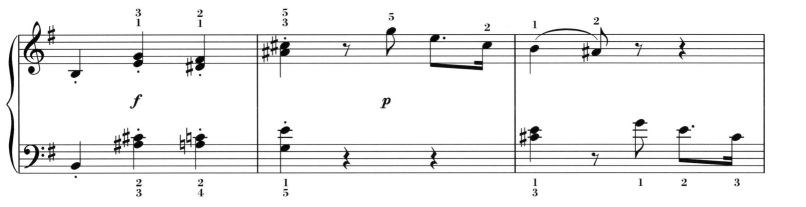

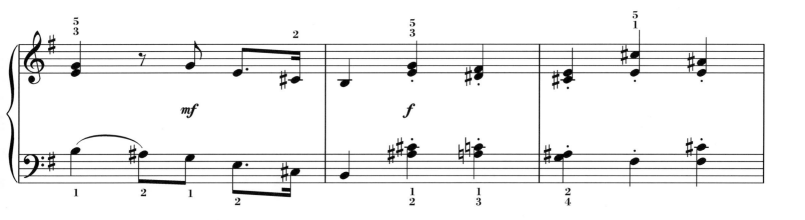

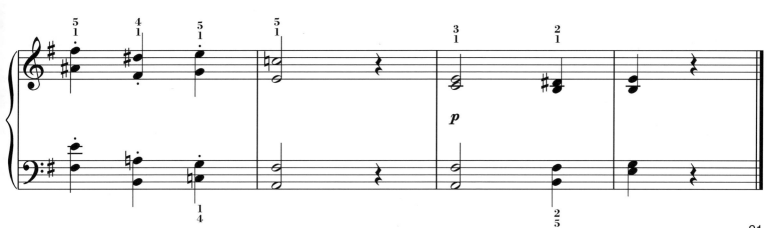

Piano Concerto No. 2

First Movement Theme

Opus 21

By Frédéric Chopin

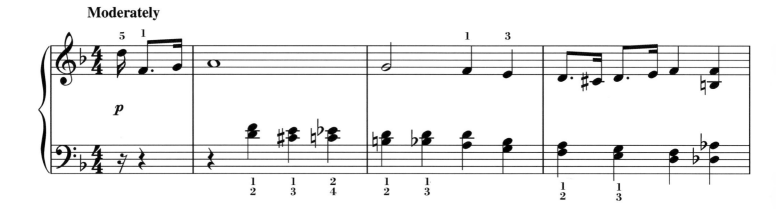

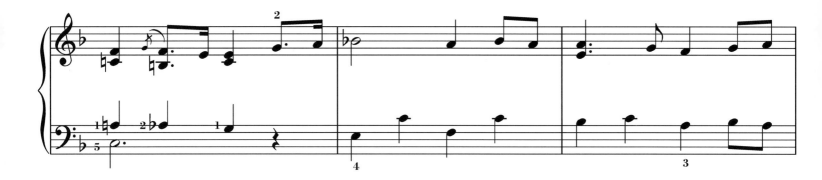

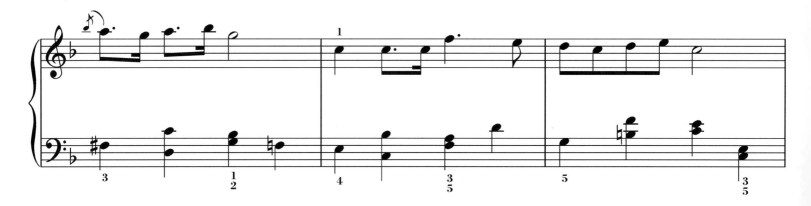

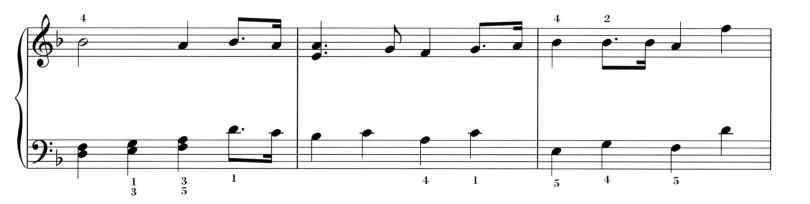

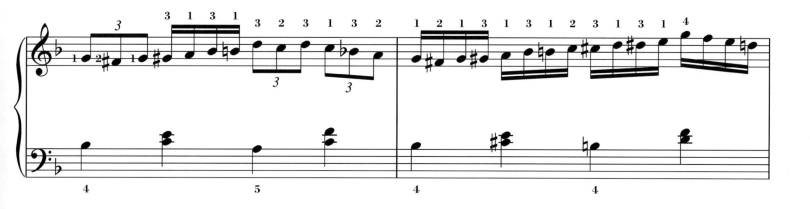

23

Piano Sonata No. 2

Third Movement, "Funeral March"

By Frédéric Chopin

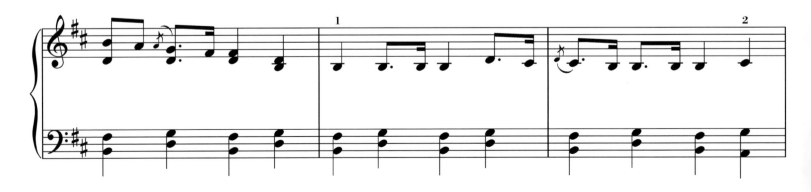

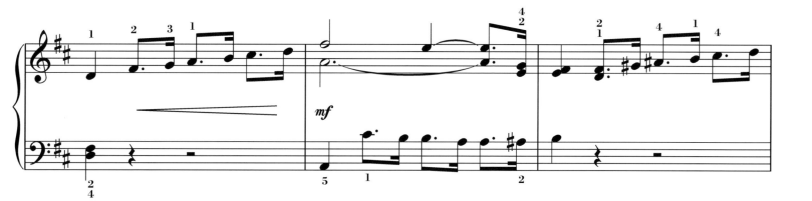

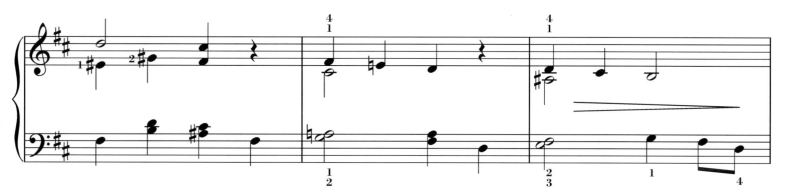

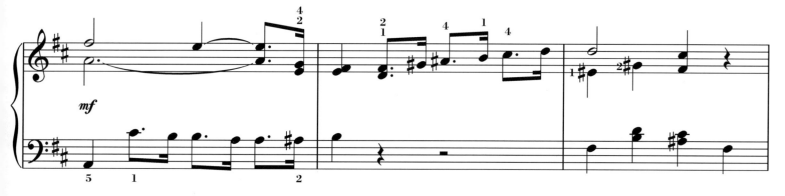

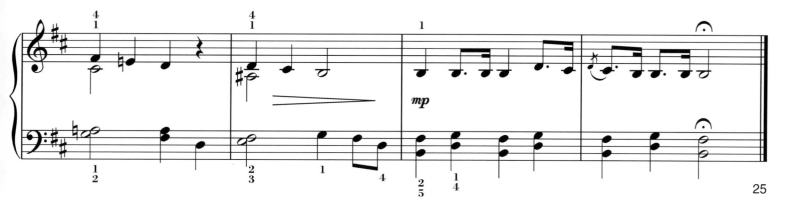

Polonaise No. 3 ("Military")

Opus 40, No. 1

By Frédéric Chopin

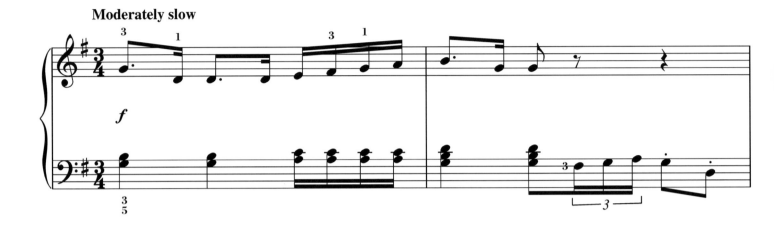

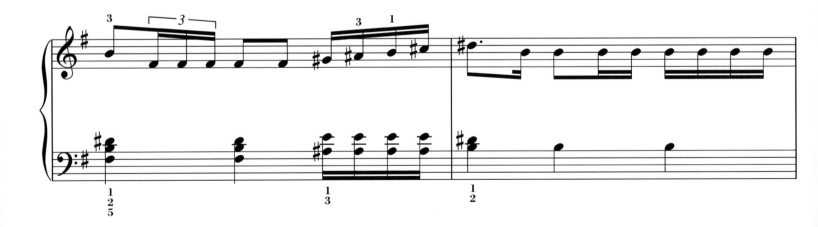

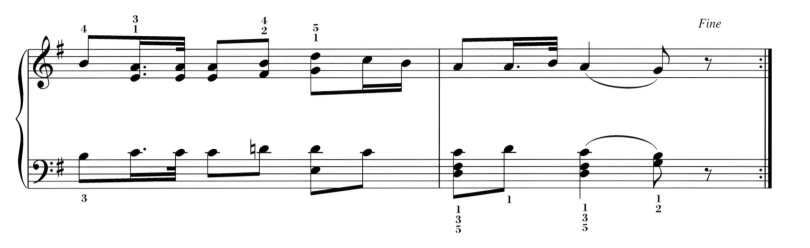

Fine

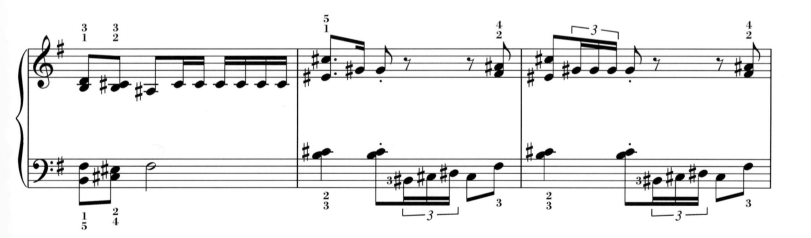

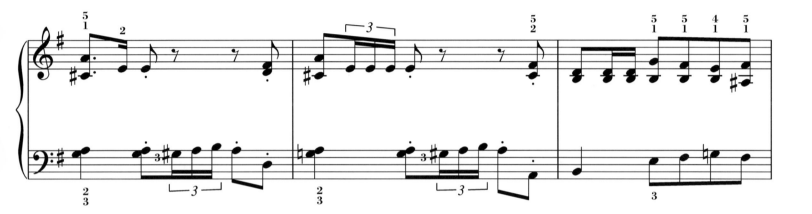

D.C. al Fine

27

Polonaise No. 6 ("Heroic")

Opus 53

By Frédéric Chopin

Moderately, majestically

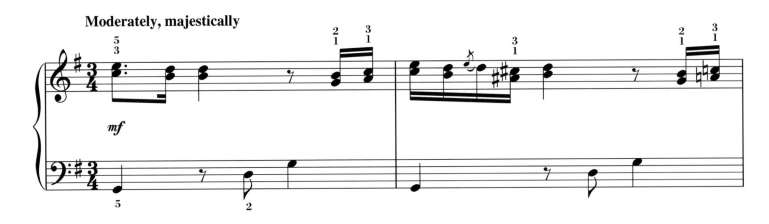

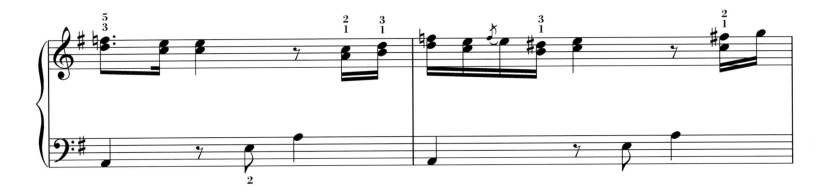

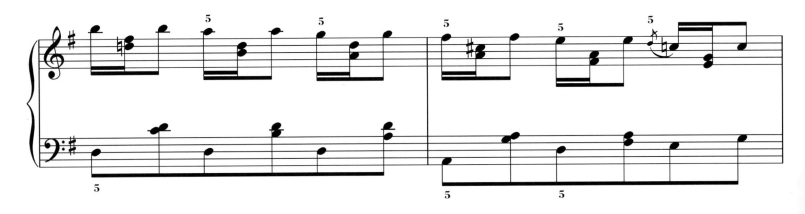

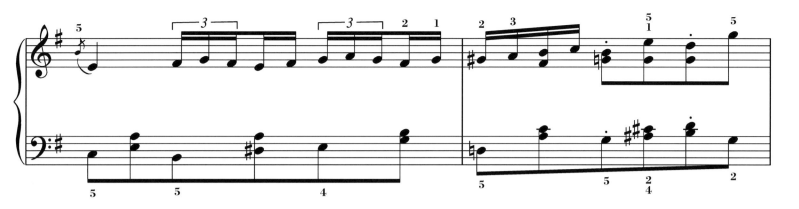

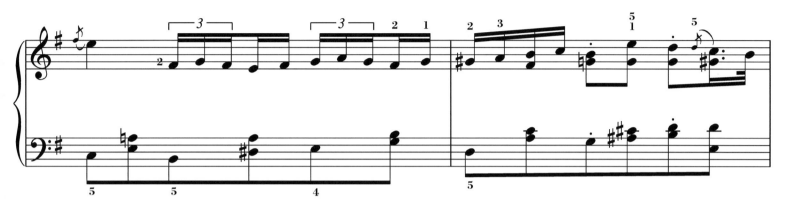

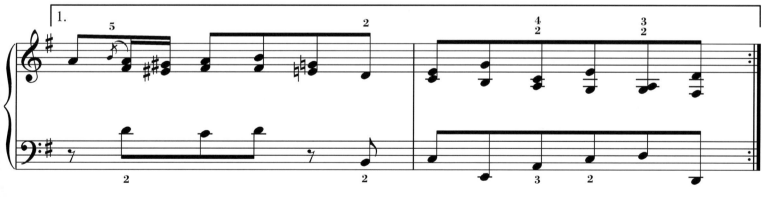

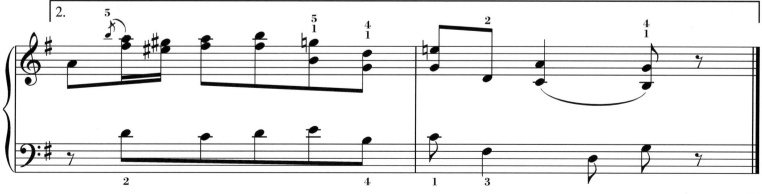

Prelude No. 4
Opus 28, No. 4

By Frédéric Chopin

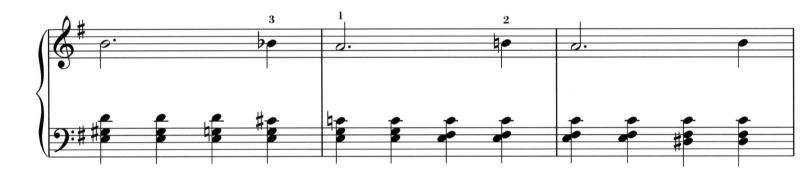

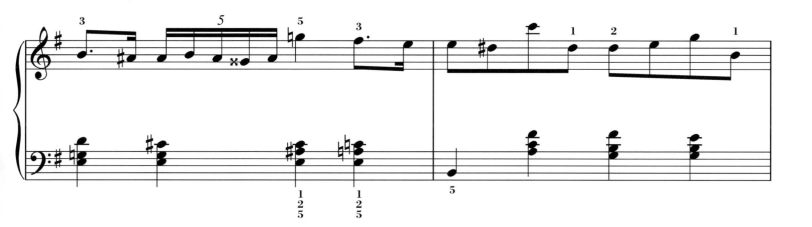

Prelude No. 7

Opus 28, No. 7

By Frédéric Chopin

Moderately slow

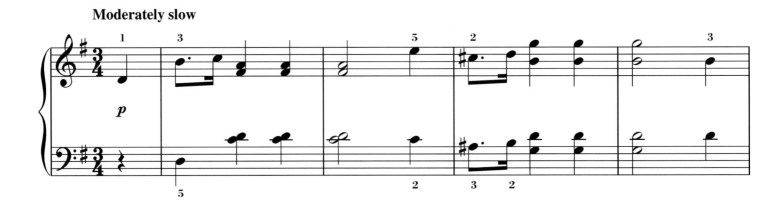

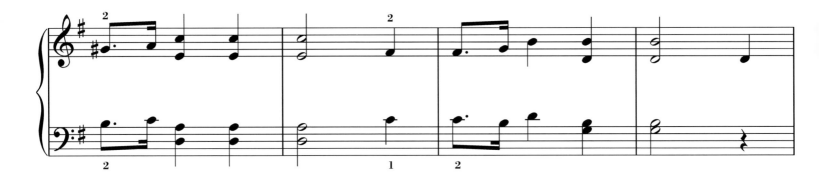

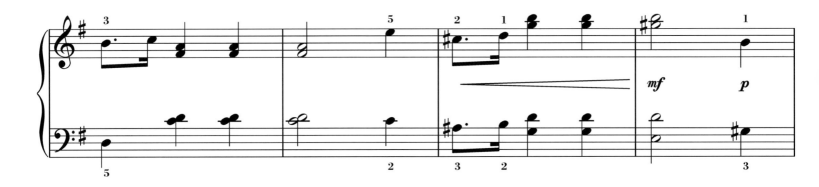

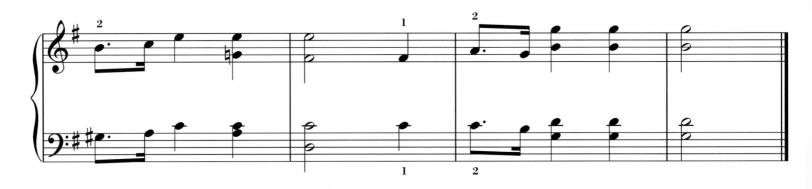

Prelude No. 20

Opus 28, No. 20

By Frédéric Chopin

Very slowly

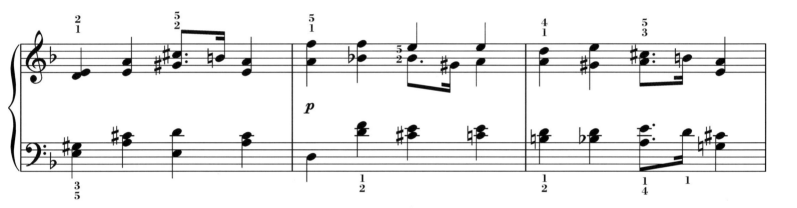

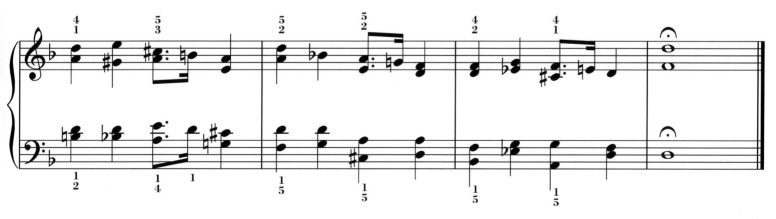

Waltz No. 3

Opus 34, No. 2

By Frédéric Chopin

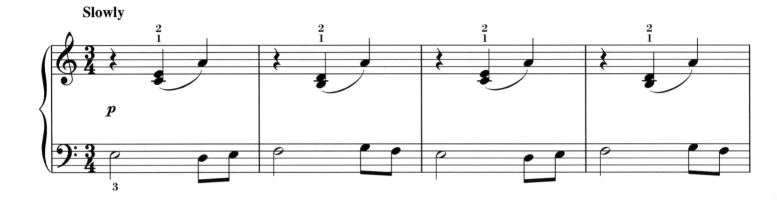

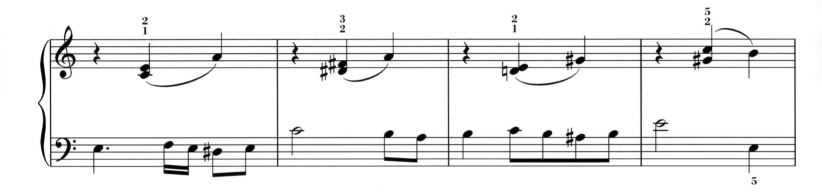

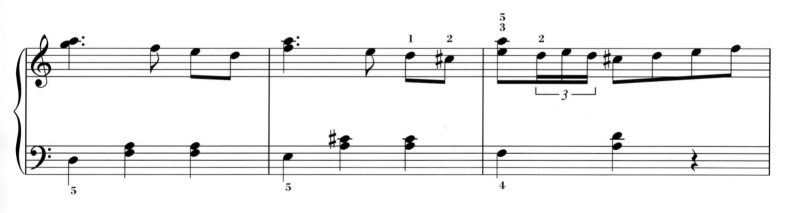

Waltz No. 7

Opus 64, No. 2

By Frédéric Chopin

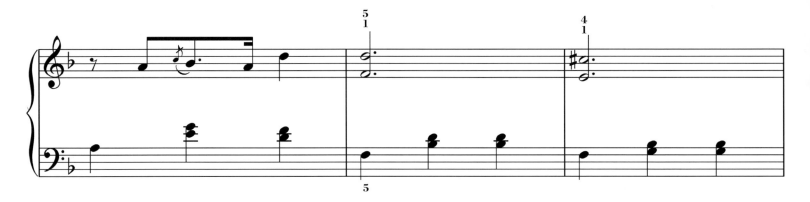

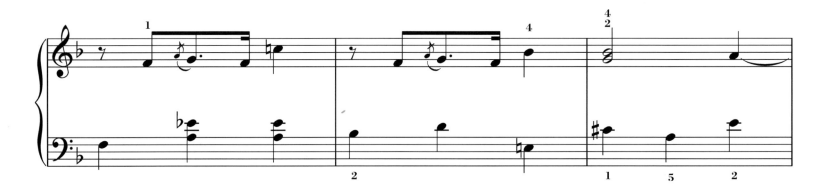

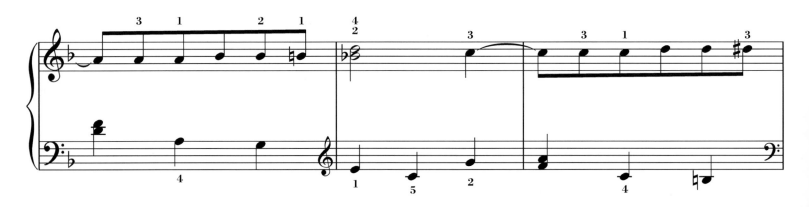

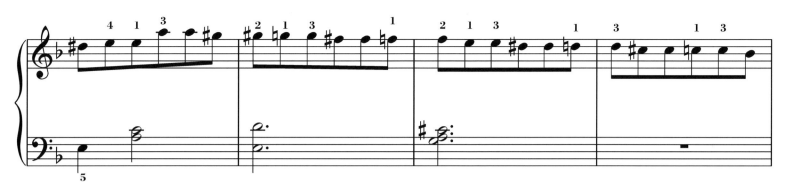

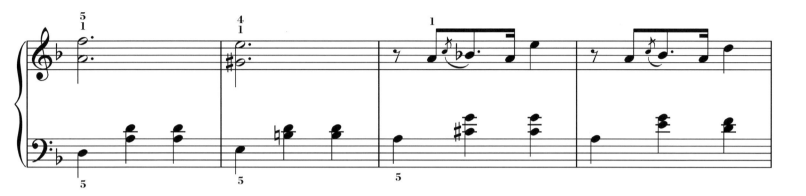

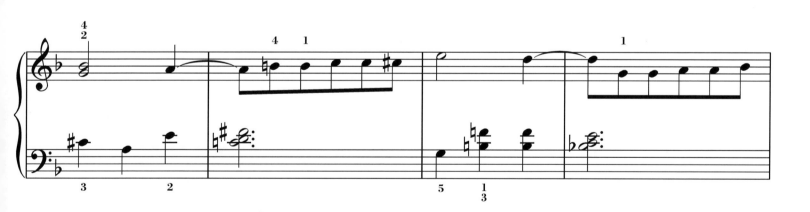

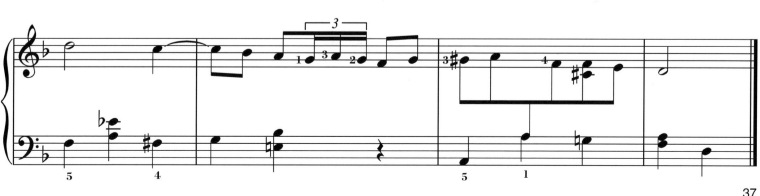

Waltz No. 15

Opus posthumous

By Frédéric Chopin

Moderately

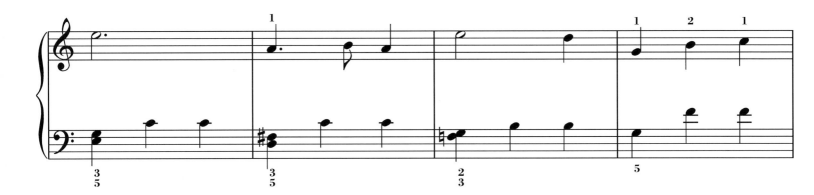

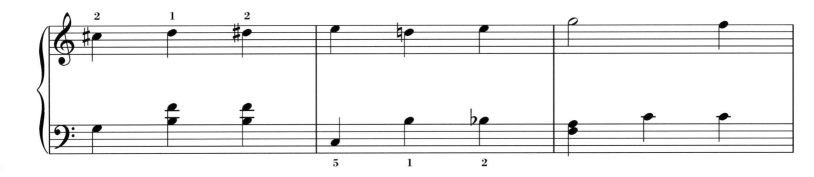

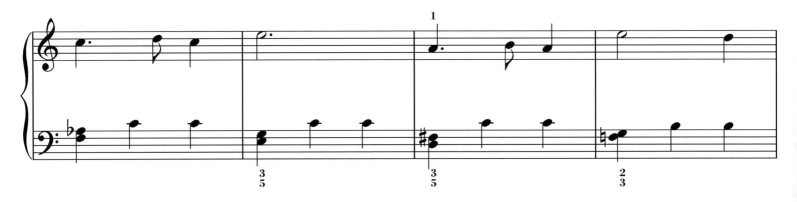

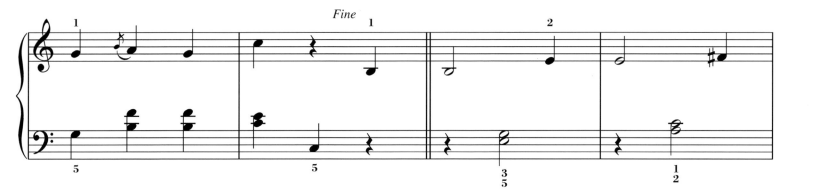

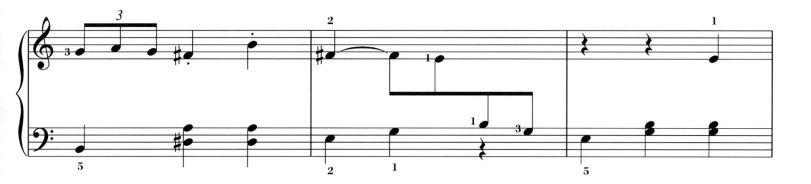

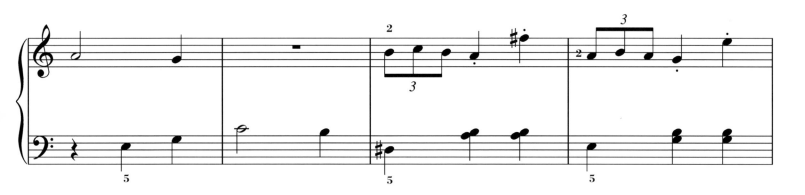

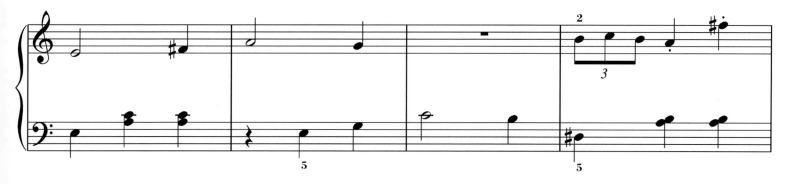

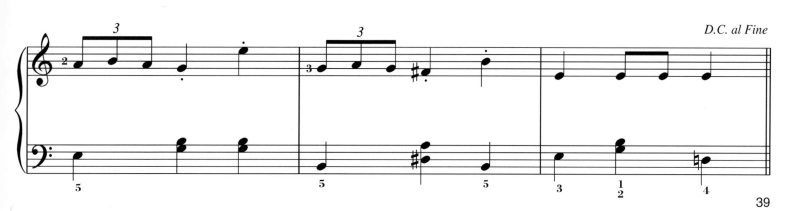

YOUR FAVORITE CLASSICAL MUSIC FOR EASY PIANO

21 Great Classics
The Phillip Keveren Series
Features 21 beloved classical masterworks by famous composers arranged for easy piano by Phillip Keveren. Includes: Air on the G String • Can Can • Canon in D Major • Eine Kleine Nachtmusik • La donna è mobile • and more.
00310717 .... $14.99

Easy Classics
18 classical masterworks from composers like Bach, Beethoven, Bizet, Brahms, Schubert, Verdi and others. Selections include: Ave Maria • Canon in D Major • Für Elise • Liebestraum • Habanera • Ode to Joy • Sicilienne • and more.
00240217 .... $8.99

The Most Beautiful Classical Melodies
46 classical favorites: Air on the G String (Bach) • Canon in D (Pachelbel) • Jesu, Joy of Man's Desiring (Bach) • Panis Angelicus (O Lord Most Holy) (Franck) • Pomp and Circumstance (Elgar) • and more.
02500095 .... $14.99

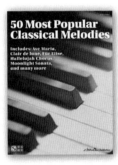

50 Easy Classical Themes
Easy arrangements of 50 classical tunes from 30 composers: Bach, Beethoven, Chopin, Debussy, Handel, Haydn, Liszt, Mozart, Puccini, Rossini, Schubert, Strauss, Tchaikovsky, Vivaldi and more.
00311215 .... $16.99

First 50 Baroque Pieces You Should Play on Piano
Includes: Air (Air on the G String) (J.S. Bach) • Jesu, Joy of Man's Desiring (J.S. Bach) • Lullaby in F Major (Kirnberger) • March in D Major (J.S. Bach) • Minuet in G Major (J.S. Bach) • more.
00291453 .... $15.99

My First Classical Song Book
34 famous classical melodies, each illustrated with color photography of great paintings. Contents: Arioso • Toccata & Fugue in D min • Fur Elise • Hungarian Dance No. 5 • Lullaby • Meditation • and more.
00312532 .... $19.99

50 Most Popular Classical Melodies
Easy arrangements of beloved pieces including: Ave Maria • By the Beautiful Blue Danube • Canon in D • Clair De Lune • Dance of the Sugar Plum Fairy • Für Elise • Hallelujah Chorus • Moonlight Sonata • and dozens of others.
02501401 .... $16.99

First 50 Classical Pieces You Should Play on the Piano
A great collection of must-know classics: Ave Maria (Schubert) • In the Hall of the Mountain King (Grieg) • Jesu, Joy of Man's Desiring (Bach) • Moonlight Sonata (Beethoven) • and more.
00131436 .... $15.99

The Piano Bench of Easy Classical Music
400 pages of great music literature, specially selected for the developing pianist. Includes: Air (Handel) • Habañera (Bizet) • Jesu, Joy of Man's Desiring (JS Bach) • Liebestraume (Liszt) • more.
14025483 .... $29.99

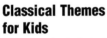

Classical Themes for Kids
25 timeless classical selections: The Flight of the Bumble Bee • Hornpipe • Liebestraum No. 3 • Pomp and Circumstance • Rhapsody in Blue • Toreador Song • William Tell Overture • more.
00346750 .... $10.99

Hooked on Easy Piano Classics
35 classics: Canon in D (Pachelbel) • The Entertainer (Joplin) • March Militaire (Schubert) • Moonlight Sonata (Beethoven) • Romeo and Juliet (Tchaikovsky) • Toreador Song (Bizet) • and more.
00004029 .... $14.99

Simple Classical Piano Pieces
Play 50 favorites by Bach, Beethoven, Mozart, and others that are perfect for beginners. Inclues: Aria • Dance In G Major • Little Rondo • Minuet • Rigaudon • Sonatina • Waltz, Op. 101, No. 1 • and more.
00288045 .... $9.99

Contemporary Piano Masters
This exceptional collection includes: Dawn from *Pride & Prejudice* (Dario Marianelli) • Fly (Ludovico Einaudi) • Game of Thrones Theme (Ramin Djawadi) • The Shape of Water Theme (Alexandre Desplat) • and more.
00290990 .... $19.99

The Library of Easy Piano Classics
A treasury of pieces that have captured the imagination of music lovers: Clair de Lune • Country Gardens • Melody in F • Pachelbel's Canon • Albeniz's Tango • and much more. Spiral bound.
14019031 .... $27.99

HAL•LEONARD®
www.halleonard.com